I0225647

The Book of Thomas
The Contender

Mystical Teachings on the Struggle for Enlightenment

A Modern Translation

Adapted for the Contemporary Reader

Thomas the Apostle
(Gnostic Tradition)

Translated by Tim Zengerink

© Copyright 2025
All rights reserved.

It is not legal to reproduce, duplicate, or transmit any part of this document in either electronic means or in printed format. Recording of this publication is strictly prohibited and any storage of this document is not allowed unless with written permission from the publisher except for the use of brief quotations in a book review.

This book contains works of fiction. Any resemblance to persons living or dead, or places, events, or locations is purely coincidental.

Table Of Contents

Preface - Message to the Reader

What If You Could Help Rebuild the Greatest Library in Human History?

Thousands of years ago, the Library of Alexandria stood as the crown jewel of human achievement — a sanctuary where the collected wisdom of every known civilization was gathered, preserved, and shared freely.

And then, it was lost.

Through fire, conquest, and the slow erosion of time, humanity lost not just books — but ideas, dreams, discoveries, and stories that could have changed the world forever.

Today, the Library of Alexandria lives again — and you are invited to be a part of its restoration.

Our mission is simple yet profound:

To rebuild the greatest library the world has ever known, and to translate all timeless works into every language and dialect, so that no seeker of knowledge is ever left behind again.

By joining our movement to rebuild the modern Library of Alexandria, you become part of an unprecedented mission:

- **Unlimited Access to the Greatest Audiobooks & eBooks Ever Written:**

  Instantly explore thousands of legendary works—Plato, Shakespeare, Jane Austen, Leo Tolstoy, and countless more. All instantly available to read or listen, placing a complete literary universe at your fingertips.

- **Beautiful Paperback & Deluxe Editions at Printing Cost**

  Own any title as an elegant paperback, deluxe hardcover, or stunning collectible boxset—offered to you at true printing cost, delivered straight to your door. Build your personal Library of Alexandria, crafted for beauty, built for durability, and worthy of proud display.

- **Fresh Translations for Modern Readers—in Every Language & Dialect**

  Enjoy timeless masterpieces reimagined in clear, contemporary language—no more outdated phrases or obscure references. Alongside the original versions, we're tirelessly translating these classics into every language and dialect imaginable, ensuring accessibility and understanding across cultures and generations.

- **Join a Global Renaissance of Literature & Knowledge**

  You directly support expanding our library, publishing deluxe editions at true cost, translating works into all global languages, and bringing humanity's greatest stories to people everywhere. By joining today, you're not just preserving a legacy of masterpieces; you set in motion a powerful wave of literary accessibility.

Become a Torchbearer of Knowledge.

Join us for free now at LibraryofAlexandria.com

Together, we will ensure that the light of human wisdom never fades again.

With gratitude and a shared love of knowledge,

The Modern Library of Alexandria Team

Visit:

www.libraryofalexandria.com

Or scan the code below:

4

Introduction

The Inner Battle and the Quest for Knowledge

The Book of Thomas the Contender is one of the most introspective and philosophically rich texts in the Gnostic tradition. Preserved among the Nag Hammadi manuscripts and attributed to Thomas the Apostle, this dialogue between Jesus and Thomas reveals a vision of the spiritual path as a battle—not against the world itself, but against ignorance, illusion, and the disordered desires of the ego. In its poetic and symbolic language, the text presents an urgent call to know oneself, to overcome attachment to the material world, and to rise into the light of divine understanding.

This is not a gospel of narrative or miracle, but of reflection and revelation. In a private and intimate setting, Jesus speaks to Thomas not as a distant Lord to a passive follower, but as a teacher to a soul ready to awaken. The conversation that unfolds is one of the deepest spiritual dialogues in early Christian literature, urging the reader not simply to believe, but to see—to know truth not as dogma, but as the unveiling of the self. The central message is clear: without inner knowledge, no true liberation is possible. The soul that fails to recognize its divine origin will remain trapped in the illusions of the flesh, mistaking shadow for light and bondage for freedom.

Jesus teaches Thomas that the greatest enemy of the soul is ignorance—not merely the absence of facts, but the deeper condition of spiritual blindness. This ignorance is rooted in forgetfulness: the soul forgets its source, its purpose, and its true identity. In place of this knowledge, it becomes consumed by external things— pleasure, pride, fear, ambition, and the ever-changing flow of sensations. It clings to the body as if it were the self, and it becomes entangled in a world that promises fulfillment but never delivers peace. Against this backdrop, Jesus challenges Thomas—and by extension, the reader—to awaken. To remember. To turn inward and rediscover the Light that was placed within before the world was formed.

The journey toward this awakening is not easy. It demands discipline, clarity, and courage. The soul must wrestle with its own confusion and confront the forces within that seek to keep it asleep. These forces are not demons in the traditional sense, but patterns of thought, emotion, and desire that veil the soul in darkness. The text speaks of the "powers" and the "rulers"—spiritual realities that stand between the soul and its ascent. But it also affirms that these can be overcome. The Light is stronger than the darkness. Truth is stronger than illusion. And the soul, once it truly sees, cannot be enslaved again.

Thomas, as the archetypal seeker, listens with reverence but also with human frailty. He asks, he hesitates, he reflects. His role is not to display perfect faith but to model the sincere struggle of the soul seeking truth. Jesus meets him with patience and urgency, revealing mysteries gradually and with deep compassion. The text makes it clear that awakening is not a gift bestowed randomly—it is the fruit of desire, discipline, and divine grace. It requires the seeker to die to the old self, to renounce false identities, and to walk the narrow path that leads to life. This is the path of the contender: the one who strives not with violence but with vision, not with conquest but with clarity.

The Gnostic Vision of the Soul's Redemption

The Gnostic tradition, from which The Book of Thomas the Contender arises, is often misunderstood. It is not a rejection of the world for its own sake, nor a denial of the body as something evil. Rather, it is a profound critique of illusion—of the ways in which the soul becomes lost in appearances and forgets its true nature. Gnosticism teaches that salvation is not escape but awakening. That the world is not inherently evil, but that its surface conceals deeper truths. And that the divine spark is hidden within each of us, waiting to be uncovered through inner knowing.

This gospel affirms these principles with clarity and force. It portrays the human condition not as a fall into sin, but as a descent into forgetfulness. The soul, once united with the divine, has become enmeshed in the material realm and distracted by its many voices. It does not know what it is, and so it suffers. It seeks satisfaction in the temporary and misses the eternal. But the path of redemption is always open. Through knowledge—gnosis—the soul remembers its source, sees through illusion, and returns to the divine fullness (pleroma) from which it came.

Jesus speaks of the body not as a prison, but as a garment. It is something we wear for a time, something that allows experience but does not define the self. To mistake the garment for the person is the essence of spiritual ignorance. The one who knows himself, however, is no longer deceived. He sees the body as part of a larger journey, and he no longer fears its decline. He lives not for the flesh but for the spirit. And in this knowledge, he is free.

This view of self-knowledge is deeply empowering. It places the responsibility for awakening within the hands of each individual. No priest or prophet can substitute for your own inner vision. No ritual or tradition can awaken the soul unless the soul itself desires to awaken. Jesus does not ask Thomas to believe blindly or to obey without question. He invites him to understand, to see, to enter into the truth that sets one free. And this invitation is extended to all who read this text today.

The Book of Thomas the Contender also contains a recurring theme of urgency. Time is short, and the soul must not delay. The world is full of distractions, and the longer we sleep, the harder it becomes to wake. Jesus warns that the world will seek to seduce, to confuse, and to control—but those who know the truth will not be fooled. They will walk in the light, live from the spirit, and speak with authority. This is not arrogance—it is the humility of one who sees clearly and acts from the center of being. The gospel reminds us that true freedom is not given—it is reclaimed.

This modern translation has been carefully prepared to preserve the symbolic and philosophical depth of the original text while making its insights fully accessible to contemporary readers. Each passage has been rendered with clarity and reverence, allowing the spiritual dialogue to speak in its own rhythm and power. Archaic phrasing has been softened, but the mystery and depth have been preserved. The goal is not only to translate the words but to carry the experience—the invitation to wake up, to see clearly, and to walk the path of wisdom.

To read this gospel is to enter a sacred encounter. It is not a text to be consumed quickly or analyzed from a distance. It is a mirror in which we see our own struggles, a voice that speaks to our deepest longings, and a guide that points beyond the surface of things. It does not offer simple answers but challenges us to undertake the inner work that leads to lasting freedom.

Let this book be a companion in your own inner journey. Let Jesus' words awaken your desire for truth. Let Thomas' questions become your own. And may you, like the contender, rise with strength and clarity to meet the spiritual path that lies before you—not as a burden, but as your birthright. In the struggle, you will find strength. In the knowing, you will find peace. And in the truth, you will remember who you truly are.

The Book of Thomas
The Contender

The hidden words spoken by the Savior to Judas Thomas, which I, Mathaias, wrote down as I walked with them, listening to their conversation.

The Savior said, "Brother Thomas, while you are still in this world, listen carefully to my words. I will reveal the answers to the thoughts you have kept inside. Since people say you are my twin and my true companion, take a moment to look within yourself. Learn who you really are, understand your existence, and discover how you have come to be. Since you are called my brother, you should not remain unaware of your true nature.

"I see that you have already begun to understand because you recognize that I bring the knowledge of truth. Even though you walk with me and do not yet fully comprehend everything, you have already started to know. Because of this, you will be called 'the one who knows himself.' For the person who does not know themselves knows nothing, but the one who comes to understand themselves also gains insight into the deep mysteries of all things. Therefore, my brother Thomas, you have seen what is hidden from most people—things that they stumble over in their ignorance."

Thomas replied, "Lord, I ask you to answer the questions I carry in my heart before you leave this world. When I hear you speak of hidden truths, I will be able to share them. But I realize now that understanding and living the truth is not easy for people."

The Savior answered, "If even the things you can see are unclear and confusing to you, how will you understand when I speak of things that are unseen? If the works of truth that are obvious in this world are already difficult for you to follow, how can you hope to carry out the actions that belong to the higher realms and the fullness of divine perfection, which are beyond human sight? How, then, will you be known as true 'workers' of the truth? For now, you are still like students who have not yet reached completion."

Thomas said to him, "Master, please tell us more about these things that are hidden from our understanding."

The Savior replied, "All living bodies, including animals, come into existence through natural birth. Their origins are clear, as is their nature. In the same way, the things that belong to the higher realms, though not visible in the same way, exist through their own roots. These roots produce fruit that sustains them. The bodies you see in this world, however, survive by consuming other living beings, creating a cycle of change. But this change leads to decay and death because these bodies do not hold the hope of eternal life. They are like the animals—they perish in the same way. If their origin is the same, how can they create anything different? This is why you are still like children until you reach a greater understanding."

Thomas then said, "This is why I say, Lord, that those who try to explain hidden and difficult matters are like people shooting arrows at a target in the dark. They aim and shoot as if they can see the target, but they do not truly know where it is. But when the light appears and removes the darkness, their efforts will become clear. And you, our light, reveal the truth to us, O Lord."

The Savior said, "Light finds its existence within light."

Thomas asked, "Lord, why does the light we see, which shines for people, rise and set every day?"

The Savior answered, "Thomas, this light exists for your sake—not so you can stay in this world forever, but so you can find your way out of it. When all who are chosen have turned away from their earthly desires, this light will return to its source, and its true essence will welcome it back because it has faithfully done its work."

The Savior continued, "Oh, the deep love of the true light! But also, how fierce is the fire that burns inside human bodies and bones! This fire is in them day and night, consuming their strength, clouding their thoughts, and leading their souls into confusion. It stirs up desires, both seen and unseen, pushing men toward women and women toward men.

"This is why it is said, 'Whoever seeks the truth from true wisdom must create wings for themselves so they can fly and escape the desires that control people.' He must rise above every earthly craving and free himself from the pull of the physical world."

Thomas said, "Lord, this is exactly what I want to understand, for I see that you are the one who brings true knowledge and guidance."

The Savior replied, "We must talk about these things because they are meant for those who are working toward perfection. If you want to be perfect, you must think about these truths and follow them. If you do not, then you will be called 'foolish,' for a wise person cannot live in harmony with someone who refuses to understand. A wise person grows in knowledge, while a fool sees no difference between good and bad. To the fool, they are the same. But the wise man is nourished by truth, and as the scripture says, 'He will be like a tree planted beside flowing water,' always growing and strengthened by the waters of life.

"But some, even though they have the ability to rise above, still chase after things they can see, things far from the truth. They are deceived by the fire that guides them—it looks like light, but it is only an illusion. This fire shines with a temporary beauty, attracting them with its charm. It tricks them with pleasure, trapping them in a false sense of happiness. It blinds them with endless desires, burning their souls with cravings they cannot escape. It is like a sharp stake driven into their hearts, something they cannot pull out.

"This fire, like a bridle in their mouths, controls them and steers their actions according to its will. It binds them with chains, wrapping itself around every part of them. It traps them in the suffering of wanting things that will fade away, things that constantly change and never satisfy. These people are pulled downward by their desires, consumed by them. In the end, they become like animals in this temporary world, no different from everything else that is destined to decay."

Thomas thought about this and said, "It is true, just as it is said, 'Many do not understand the truth of their own soul.'"

The Savior answered, "Blessed is the wise person who searches for truth. When he finds it, he will rest in it forever. No one will be able to shake him or make him afraid, for he will be standing on a foundation that cannot be moved."

Thomas then asked, "Lord, is it good for us to stay among people who are like us?"

The Savior said, "Yes, it is good to find peace among those who share the truth. The things people see and hold onto in this world will not last forever. Their bodies will break down and return to the earth, just like everything else that is physical. When that happens, the fire they once feared will become their suffering, fueled by their attachment to their old way of life. They will be trapped by what is visible, unable to rise beyond it.

"And those who look toward the unseen but do not truly love the truth will also perish. Their focus on worldly things will consume them, and the fire within them will destroy their souls. Soon, all that can be seen will fade away, and from its remains, only empty shadows will rise—lost souls. These souls will remain in suffering, clinging to lifeless bodies, tormented by corruption and despair."

Thomas asked, "What should we say to these people? How can we speak to those who cannot see the truth? What message should we share with those who say, 'We came to do good, not to bring curses,' yet also claim, 'If we had not been born into the flesh, we would not have known sin'?"

The Savior answered, "You must not think of such people as truly human. They are like wild animals, consuming each other with their actions. They are blind to the kingdom of light because they are drawn to the deceptive sweetness of the fire. They serve death, rushing toward corruption, following the desires of those who came before them—those who sought destruction. These people will fall into the abyss, where they will suffer the consequences of their wickedness. They will be overcome with confusion and despair, wanting to escape their own bodies but unable to do so peacefully.

"They take pleasure in their own madness without realizing it. They blindly follow their own distorted thinking, convinced they are wise. Their entire being— body, mind, and soul—is consumed by their selfish desires. They focus only on their own actions, but in the end, the fire will devour them. It will burn away their illusions, leaving them in great suffering."

Thomas asked, "Lord, what will happen to those who are cast down among them? My heart is heavy because many struggle against them."

The Savior looked at him and said, "What do you think, Thomas? What is your own understanding?"

Judas, called Thomas, answered, "Lord, it is for you to speak, and for me to listen and learn."

The Savior replied, "Then listen carefully and believe in the truth of what I say. Both the one who plants the seed and the seed itself will pass away, for everything must go through the fire. Both fire and water will consume them, and they will find themselves trapped in darkness. Over time, they will bear the bitter fruit of wickedness. Their judgment will come, and they will be destroyed by the very things they once fed—the beasts, the people, and even the forces of nature: the rain, the wind, the air, and the light above."

Thomas said, "Lord, your words have convinced us. We know in our hearts that they are true. But the world will not understand them. To them, your words will sound foolish, even laughable. How, then, can we go out and teach these things? The world does not respect us."

The Savior said, "I tell you the truth, those who hear your words but turn away in mockery, who laugh at the truth you share, will not escape judgment. Such people will be handed over to the ruler above, the one who has power over all others. This ruler will cast them down from heaven into the abyss, where they will be trapped in darkness, unable to move or escape. The depths of suffering will surround them, and there will be no forgiveness, no relief from their torment.

"The angel of punishment, Tartarouchos, will chase them, striking them with whips of fire that send sparks into their faces. No matter where they run, the fire will follow them. If they try to flee west, the flames will block their way. If they turn south, the fire will rise before them. If they go north, the burning heat will still be there. Even if they turn east, they will find no escape, for they did not seek refuge while they were alive. How will they find it when the day of judgment arrives?"

The Savior continued, "How terrible it will be for those who live without hope, who trust in things that will never come true.

"How terrible for those who put their faith in the flesh and cling to this dying world! How long will you remain blind? How long will you foolishly believe that what is eternal will also pass away? You have tied your hope to this world, and you treat this short life as your god! By doing so, you have ruined your own souls.

"How terrible for those consumed by the fire of desire, for it will never be satisfied.

"How terrible for those trapped in an endless cycle of struggle, unable to break free.

"How terrible for those who are burned by desires that destroy their bodies and poison their souls. These flames prepare them for a dreadful fate alongside others who will suffer the same."

How terrible for those who are prisoners in the darkness they have chosen! You laugh, but your laughter is empty. Your joy is wild and meaningless. You do not even realize your own downfall. You do not stop to think about your condition. You do not see that you live in darkness and walk in the shadow of death. Instead, you are consumed by the fire within you, fooled by its illusion of warmth and comfort. You have been blinded by your own desires, taking pleasure in the very things that destroy you. You find sweetness in the poison that is killing you, and you welcome the suffering caused by your own choices. You have traded freedom for chains, filling your hearts with emptiness and your minds with foolish thoughts. The fire of your own making has surrounded you with smoke, hiding the light from your eyes. You have wrapped yourselves in falsehood, trusting in things that will never last.

Do you not see that you live among those who seek to harm you? They do not see you as equals but as something to use. You have washed your souls in the water of darkness, following your desires without realizing the traps all around you. How terrible for you who have chosen lies over truth! You fail to understand that the sun, which sees everything, is watching and will one day bring justice. Even the moon sees what happens in the night and day, witnessing the actions of all people.

How terrible for those who chase after fleeting pleasures, letting their desires rule over them. How terrible for those who let their own bodies control them, for these desires will only bring suffering. How terrible for those who give in to evil spirits, letting their passions burn uncontrollably. Who will bring cool water to quench their inner fire? Who will shine a light to break the darkness inside them? Who will cleanse the polluted waters of their soul?

The sun, the moon, the air, the spirit, the earth, and the water all give life to the world. But if the sun does not shine on these things, they will dry up and die like weeds. The weeds grow wild and unchecked, choking out everything good around them. But when the grapevine is planted, it grows strong and spreads its shade over the land. It overtakes the weeds and brush, turning the soil into something rich and full of life. The vine grows healthy and full, bringing joy to its master, who no longer has to struggle against the weeds. The vine restores the land, making it fertile and abundant.

Jesus continued, saying, "How terrible for those who have rejected the truth! You work hard, but without understanding, and you rush toward your own destruction. You try to silence those who speak about life and truth, but even when you kill them, they rise again to testify against your ways.

"Blessed are those who see the dangers ahead and turn away from them.

"Blessed are those who suffer rejection and mockery because they love the Lord.

"Blessed are those who weep under the weight of suffering, for they will be set free and find peace.

"Stay alert and pray, so you do not remain trapped in the flesh. Break free from the chains of bitterness that tie you to this world. In prayer, you will find rest, leaving behind the pain and shame of this life. When you are freed from the struggles and desires of the body, you will enter the eternal rest that the Good One has prepared for you. You will reign with the King, united with him as he is with you, now and forever."

The Book of Thomas the Contender ends with this:

Remember me, my brothers and sisters, in your prayers. Peace be with the saints and with all who walk in the Spirit.

Thank You for Reading

Dear Reader,

We hope this timeless classic has sparked your imagination and enriched your literary journey. Now that you've turned the final page, we want to share a vision for the future of reading—one where every classic you've ever wanted to explore is at your fingertips, in a format that best suits your life.

We'd like to invite you to gain immediate, unlimited digital & audiobook access to hundreds of the most treasured literary classics ever written—along with the option to secure deluxe paperback, hardcover & box set editions at printing cost. Together, we can spark a new global literary renaissance alongside our small, independent publishing house called "The Library of Alexandria."

Thousands of years ago, the Library of Alexandria stood as a beacon of knowledge—until it was lost to history. We aim to reignite that spirit of preservation and discovery right now, in the modern age—only this time, it's accessible to all, in every language and every format.

Picture a world where every timeless classic, novel, poem, or philosophical treatise is not only available to read but also updated for today's readers—modernized, translated into any language or dialect, and ready to enjoy in any format you choose, whether that is in an eBook, audiobook, paperback, or deluxe hardcover & box set version a printing cost.

By joining our movement to rebuild the modern Library of Alexandria, you become part of an unprecedented mission to offer:

- **Unlimited Audiobook & eBook Access to the Greatest Classics of All Time**

  Instantly explore thousands of legendary works, from Plato and Shakespeare to Jane Austen and Leo Tolstoy. All are instantly ready to read or listen to, giving you a complete literary universe at your fingertips.

- **Paperback & Deluxe Editions at Printing Costs:**

  Purchase any title in a paperback, deluxe hardbound, or deluxe boxset edition at printing costs, shipped right to your doorstep. Curate your personal library of Alexandria with editions worthy of display— crafted to last, designed to captivate, and delivered straight to your door.

- **Modern translations for Contemporary Readers in all languages and dialects**

  Discover a vast selection of classics reimagined in clear, current language—no more struggling with outdated phrases or obscure references. Next to the original versions, we aim to offer translations in as many languages and dialects as possible.

  As we continue our translation efforts and add new languages, readers everywhere can connect with these works as if they were written today. By bridging linguistic divides, you're contributing to ensuring that these timeless stories become more meaningful, accessible, and inspiring for people across the globe.

- **Your Personal Library of Alexandria:**

  Over the months and years, you'll curate a unique physical archive of classics—each volume a testament to your taste, curiosity, and love of knowledge. It's not just about owning books—it's about curating a cultural legacy you'll cherish and pass down for generations to come.

- **Join a Global Literary Renaissance:**

  Your support fuels an ongoing mission: allowing us to reinvest in offering deluxe print editions (including special boxsets) at their true cost, broaden the range of available formats and translations, and extend the reach of these works to new audiences worldwide. By joining today, you're not just preserving a legacy of masterpieces; you set in motion a powerful wave of literary accessibility.

We are more than a publisher—we're a movement, and we can't do it alone. Your support lets us scale our mission, preserving and reimagining history's greatest works for tomorrow's readers.

Become a Torchbearer of knowledge.

Thank you for picking up this book and allowing us into your literary journey. As you turn the pages, know that you're part of something larger: a global effort to keep these stories alive, share their wisdom across borders and generations, and spark a true cultural revival for the modern era.

If this resonates with you—please consider taking the next step by visiting:

www.libraryofalexandria.com

With gratitude and a shared love of knowledge,

The Modern Library of Alexandria Team

Visit:

www.libraryofalexandria.com

Or scan the code below:

www.ingramcontent.com/pod-product-compliance
Lightning Source LLC
Chambersburg PA
CBHW010237100426
42813CB00012B/2637

* 9 7 8 1 8 0 4 2 1 6 3 5 4 *